There was a time, not so long ago, when major-league baseball players were normal everyday people, just like you and me. Back then, ballplayers weren't multimillionaires, and many of them lived in the neighborhoods where they played.

From the East Bronx, where I grew up, my buddies and I used to ride the subways to Yankee Stadium, Ebbets Field, and the Polo Grounds to cheer for our hometown heroes as they pitched shutouts, made acrobatic catches, and hit tape measure home runs.

With just three days' lunch money, you could purchase two subway tokens and a seat in the bleachers, and have enough left over to buy a hot dog at the game. Then, after the final pitch, you'd wait by the clubhouse door, and when the players stepped out onto the sidewalk, they'd stop to chat with you, playing catch, giving hitting and fielding pointers, and answering your questions about bunting, throwing, sliding, or anything else.

SAY-HEY AND THE BABE

TWO MOSTLY TRUE BASEBALL STORIES

NEIL WALDMAN

HOLIDAY HOUSE / NEW YORK

For Jan Cheripko, fellow ballplayer, writer, and friend, who encouraged and needled me, insisting that these two stories should be blended, and turned into a book

The monotone illustrations are rendered in pen and ink and the color illustrations are rendered in watercolor, acrylic, and graphite, both on Arches hotpressed watercolor paper.

The sidebar illustration entitled "The Fifties" is © New York Daily News, L.P. reprinted with permission.

Copyright © 2006 by Neil Waldman
All Rights Reserved
Printed in the United States of America
www.holidayhouse.com
First Edition
1 3 5 7 9 10 8 6 4 2

Library of Congress Cataloging-in-Publication Data
Waldman, Neil.
Say-Hey and the Babe : two mostly true baseball stories / by Neil Waldman.
p. cm.
Summary: Presents two interrelated stories, based on fact, about the 1927 New York Yankees,
the 1951 New York Giants, and a stickball team from the Bronx. Sidebars explain
baseball terms and events of the time periods, players' nicknames, and stickball lore.
ISBN 0-8234-1857-X (hardcover)
[1. Baseball—Fiction. 2. New York (N.Y.)—History—1898-1951—Fiction.] I. Title.

PZ7.W146Say 2006
[Fic]—dc22
2004052280

ISBN-13: 978-0-8234-1857-2
ISBN-10: 0-8234-1857-X

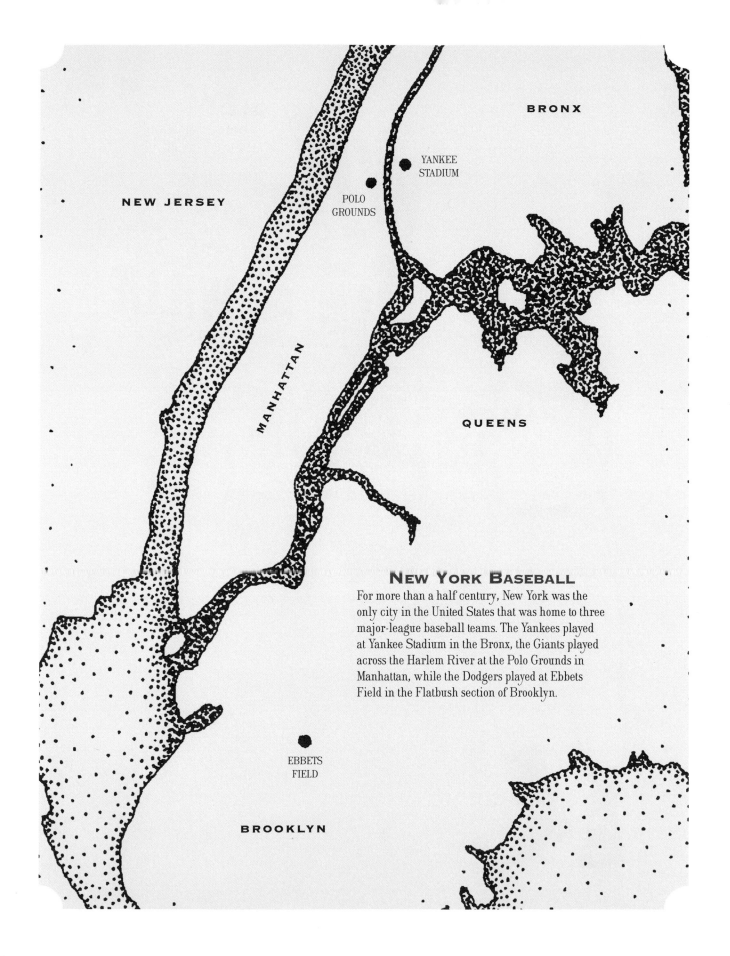

BRONX

YANKEE
STADIUM

NEW JERSEY

POLO
GROUNDS

MANHATTAN

QUEENS

NEW YORK BASEBALL

For more than a half century, New York was the
only city in the United States that was home to three
major-league baseball teams. The Yankees played
at Yankee Stadium in the Bronx, the Giants played
across the Harlem River at the Polo Grounds in
Manhattan, while the Dodgers played at Ebbets
Field in the Flatbush section of Brooklyn.

EBBETS
FIELD

BROOKLYN

INTRODUCTION

It's not easy to categorize these "mostly true" baseball stories, as they exist in a kind of no-man's land, somewhere between the genres of fiction and nonfiction. Although both stories are based on actual events I learned about during my boyhood, I've used them as launching pads for my storyteller's imagination. For that reason I've included sidebars so that you'll be able to separate fact from fancy.

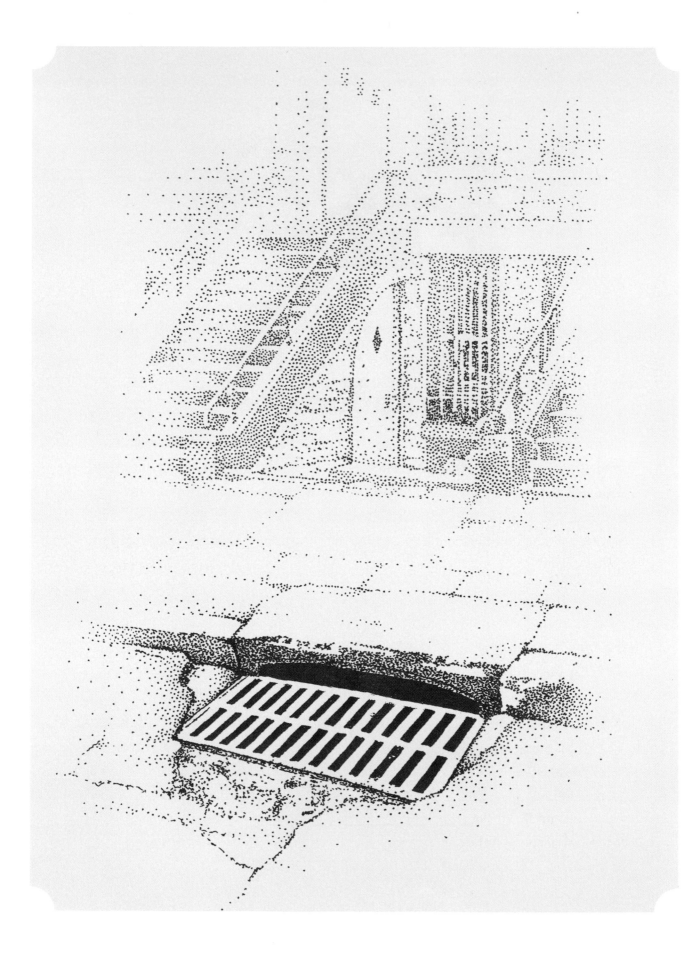

SEPTEMBER 4, 1951

PETE HUNG UPSIDE DOWN, SUSPENDED in the blackness. With his heart pounding and blood rushing to his head, he clung to the rusty iron rungs of the sewer wall. A smell like rotten cheese filled his nostrils, and Pete tried hard not to vomit. He shuddered as slime dripped onto his hair from the pipe just above him. As he descended, Pete glanced back up at his teammates holding on to both his ankles, and he began coughing.

"You aw-right, Buddy?" Moose yelled down, his voice exploding in Pete's ears.

"Yeah . . . sure," Pete answered between coughs. "I'm fine."

As he neared the sewer's bottom, freezing liquid oozed through the cracked soles of his sneakers and ran down his legs. Pete wiggled his toes, and he could feel that the slimy water had reached even there. Holding a straightened wire coat hanger with a small loop at its end, Pete reached down and began dredging the foul-smelling sewer bottom. Corralling something, he lifted a slippery leather object out of the puddle. Examining it with his fingers, Pete realized that it was an old, mud-encrusted baseball.

THE HOUSE THAT RUTH BUILT

Yankee Stadium opened in April 1923, and it was soon known as the
"House That Ruth Built" because Ruth had brought in so many fans
that the owners were able to build the new stadium. Its short right-field
fence was tailor-made for Babe Ruth's left-handed home run swing.

OPENING DAY, 1927

A BIG, ROUND-FACED MAN wearing a bow tie and a straw hat made his way through the crowded grandstands of Yankee Stadium on that cloudless April afternoon. Shaking the hands of adoring fans as he passed, he came upon a group of children, sat down, and lifted a young boy onto his lap.

"Is there anything I can do for you, little man?" he asked.

The boy remained silent.

"If you could have anything in the whole, wide world," the man urged, "what would it be?"

The boy's face broke into a smile.

"Actually, I'd love a frankfurter," he said at last.

The big man stood up and motioned to a vendor, who quickly arrived at his side.

"Let's have a hot dog for every one of these kids," he said.

Twenty minutes later, nine players trotted out onto the sparkling lawn of Yankee Stadium. The big man took his position in right field. Removing his cap, he placed it over his heart as the national anthem blared from the loudspeakers. Then the crowd cheered, and George Herman Ruth turned to face the game's first batter.

Through four-and-a-half innings, thousands of fans twisted in their seats and tapped their fingers. Not a single run had crossed home plate. Then, in the bottom of the fifth, the Bronx Bombers mounted the game's first threat. After a Philadelphia error filled the bases, more than seventy-five thousand pairs of eyes turned to the on-deck circle. One hundred and fifty thousand clapping hands shook the stadium. A sea of mouths opened wide and let out a deafening roar . . . for George Herman Ruth, the Great Bambino, was striding up to home plate with a chance to break the game wide open.

The mighty slugger dug his cleats into the red clay of the batter's box. He took two deliberate practice swings and stared into the eyes of Lefty Grove, the Athletics pitcher. The ocean of cheering voices hushed. Suddenly the ball was a blur. It streaked toward the inside corner of the plate, exploded off the Babe's bat, and rocketed toward the right-field grandstands.

As it neared the upper deck, the ball hooked into foul territory and struck a young girl on the forehead. Seventy-five thousand fans gasped as the girl slumped forward and collapsed over the railing.

THE GREAT BAMBINO

The Great Bambino is a nickname that was affectionately given to George Herman Ruth by the Italian-American community. Ruth had many other nicknames, including the Sultan of Swat and, most recognizably, the Babe.

THE 1927 BRONX BOMBERS

After their opening day victory, the Yanks went on to set an American League record for the most victories in a season (110–44) and won the pennant by nineteen games over the second-place Philadelphia Athletics. In the World Series they swept the Pirates in four straight games. Babe Ruth broke his own home run record with 60 round-trippers. Lou Gehrig won the Most Valuable Player Award, batting .373 with 47 homers and 175 RBIs. In fact, the only offensive categories in which the Yankees did not lead the league were doubles and stolen bases.

From home plate, Babe Ruth peered up into the grandstands. He stood motionless as two policemen raced to the girl's side, carefully lifted her limp body, and disappeared through an exit gate. The Babe stepped out of the batter's box, took a handkerchief from his pocket, and wiped his brow. Three pitches later, the Babe had struck out . . . but no matter. The Yanks prevailed, 8–3.

After the game the Yankee players returned to the clubhouse to find the young girl lying on a massage table. Her eyes were glazed, and the team doctor was standing over her. The Babe approached and rested a hand on the doctor's shoulder.

"Don't worry, Babe," the doctor assured him. "It's going to hurt for a couple of days; but in no time, she'll be as good as new."

"I'm mighty sorry, folks," the big man said to the girl and her father. "Listen, how'd you like a ball signed by the whole team?"

Bernard Finkel's eyes widened, a smile spreading across his face.

From around the clubhouse, Yankee players stood up and gathered around Mona and Bernard. Babe handed a ball and a pen to Lou Gehrig, who passed them to Earle Combs. One by one, the Yankees signed the ball; and then Babe placed it in Mona's hand.

"A token of our appreciation," the Babe announced, smiling from ear to ear. He gently kissed Mona's cheek, shook Bernard's hand, and escorted them out of the stadium.

As they stepped into a subway car and began

riding home, Bernard Finkel pulled the ball out of his pocket and held it between his fingers.

"You know, sweetie," he said, and smiled, "that Bambino is one terrific mensch!"

NEW YORK WORDS

Mensch is a New York word that comes from Yiddish, the language of Jewish immigrants from Europe. A mensch is a good guy, a decent person, and someone people look up to. A bambino is a young boy in Italian. *Finito la comedia* means "the play is over," also in Italian; it has a rather humorous and slightly sarcastic connotation. To schmooze means "to chat, or converse in a light-hearted way" in Yiddish.

May 5, 1927

BERNARD FINKEL BOUGHT A SPECIAL glass container for the ball, giving it a place of honor on the center of the living-room mantel . . . but it was destined to remain there for less than a month. On a steamy Saturday afternoon, Mona's brother, Harry, was playing ball with some boys in a vacant lot near 135th Street. His best friend, Leonardo Sinopoli, hit a long drive that sailed over the outfielders' heads, landing in some bushes across the street. After Leonardo rounded the bases, one of the fielders called out to the others.

"It's lost," he yelled, and the players from both teams converged on the bushes. They spent a long time searching, but the ball seemed to have vanished. After a while, they returned to the curb and sat down.

"I guess that's it, bambinos." Leonardo winked. *Finito la comedia.*
Just then Harry looked up, smiling.

"Hey, I've got a ball!" he announced. "Be back in a flash!"

Harry raced down the block and charged into his apartment house. He flew up four flights of stairs, pushed open the door, and stepped into the living room. Approaching the mantel, he lifted the glass container that held his father's special ball and snatched it.

Moments later the game resumed.

All was going well until the sixth inning, when Leonardo stepped up to the plate. After swinging wildly and missing the first pitch, he cocked his bat and launched another long drive. The ball shot past the outfielders and sailed down 135th Street. It bounced under a parked car and headed toward a sewer near the corner of Lenox Avenue.

"Oh . . . no," Harry whispered, as he watched the ball roll into the sewer and disappear.

"Well, this time you really finished us," one of the kids mumbled to Leonardo.

"Sorry, bambinos." Leonardo shrugged with a twinkle in his eyes. "Next time I'll try not to hit it so far!"

But Harry didn't even hear Leonardo's words. He just stood there in silence, staring down into the black depths of the sewer.

Then from down the block, a booming voice broke the silence.

"Haa–rrry! Get over heeeere!"

STICKBALL

In 1929 the stock market crashed, and during the depression that followed an urbanized form of baseball swept across the streets and school yards of New York. Parents scratched to save their pennies, and kids played with broomsticks instead of bats. In place of baseballs, they used rubber balls called Spauldeens that could be purchased for a dime at any local candy store. Every neighborhood had its own rules. Hits were usually measured by the number of sewers the ball traveled on the fly. One sewer was a single; two, a double; three, a triple; and four, a home run. The biggest, strongest hitters were known as Five Sewer Men. The game was called stickball.

OCTOBER 22, 1938

HARRY FINKEL AND LEONARDO SINOPOLI remained best friends throughout the Great Depression. They entered City College together; and after graduation they married their childhood sweethearts, who were both named Ruthie. Harry and Ruthie Finkel rented a small apartment on Vyse Avenue in the East Bronx; and two years later, on a chilly October morning, Ruthie gave birth to a baby boy they named Peter.

September 4, 1951

PETER FINKEL GREW UP PLAYING stickball on the streets and in the school yards of the East Bronx. He loved the way it felt when a sharp line drive exploded off his broomstick. He loved sprinting around the bases and beating the pitcher's tag at home plate. And he loved corralling long fly balls just like his hero, Willie Mays. Pete and his best friends, Moose and Eddie, formed a three-man stickball team they named the Monarchs, and they soon began competing in stickball tournaments around the city.

WILLIE

In 1951 a Giants rookie named Willie Mays arrived in New York. After games at the Polo Grounds, Willie would return to his rented room in Harlem and play stickball with the kids there. One afternoon Willie got so wrapped up in a stickball game that he forgot to make it to the Polo Grounds in time for the opening pitch. Leo Durocher, the Giants manager, sent a coach to Harlem; and when he found Willie, the star center fielder was shagging fly balls with a bunch of kids on 155th Street.

STICKBALL STYLES

There were many different ways to play stickball. Fungo was a street game played without a pitcher. The batter would lob the ball into the air and hit it before it landed, or on the bounce. But in some neighborhoods kids played a game called Slow Pitch with a pitcher who would lob the ball on one bounce toward the batter, putting as much spin on it as he could. He'd throw knuckleballs and curves by squeezing the Spauldeen before he released it, making it bounce sharply to the left or right.

In the city's school yards, the game was called Wall Ball or Pitching In. The strike zone was drawn in chalk on a wall. The pitcher would throw the ball on the fly as fast as he could.

One afternoon, during a game in Queens, a kid from the opposing team approached the Monarchs and announced that Willie Mays had begun playing stickball.

"He hops the subway after Giants games," the kid explained, "and rides to Harlem to play with the kids there."

"We've gotta find a way to go watch Willie play!" Pete insisted, and within minutes a plan was hatched.

That Wednesday none of the Monarchs bought lunch at school. They kept the thirty-five cents in their pockets and went hungry until they got home in the afternoon. They did the same thing on Thursday, and again on Friday.

SPAULDEENS

Among the old stickball players I interviewed, there wasn't one who knew why the rubber balls they played with were called "Spauldeens" instead of "Spaldings." This is a bit hard to figure as the name of the company that manufactured them, the Spalding Company, was clearly printed on the cover of every single ball.

On Saturday morning Pete gulped down his breakfast, said good-bye to his mother, and trotted out onto the sidewalk, heading toward the subway station at East 180th Street. When he arrived, Moose and Eddie were waiting for him. They each paid fifteen cents for tokens, climbed the long, metal stairway to the elevated platform, and hopped onto the number 5 train. As Pete sat watching the buildings of the Bronx whiz by, he felt his heart pounding. He was really going to see Willie play!

At the East Tremont Avenue station, two Dodgers players stepped onto the train. They sat down and started schmoozing with a group of fans.

Pete recognized them immediately. They were Pee Wee Reese and Jackie Robinson, arch rivals of his beloved Giants.

"Dem Bums're gonna get shellacked today!" Moose whispered to his teammates. "When our Jints're finished wid 'em, their gloves'll look like they wuz made outa Swiss cheese!"

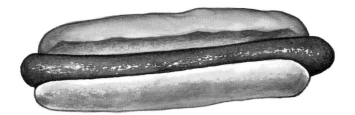

At The Polo Grounds

THE MONARCHS ARRIVED AT THE Polo Grounds, paid fifty cents for bleacher seats, and excitedly made their way through the shadows beneath the grandstands. Entering a long, dark tunnel, Pete was enticed by the mouth-watering smells of mustard and sauerkraut.

"Hey, getcha hot dogs! . . . Getcha red-hot hot dogs!" a vendor's cry echoed in the tunnel.

The Monarchs stepped out into the sunlight, and the roar of the crowd exploded in their ears.

Pete looked around wide-eyed at the exquisitely kept field. He marveled at the glistening chalk lines of the batter's boxes, the emerald green of the outfield, and the sparkling white bases that defined the great ball yard. And there, standing proudly on the perfect manicured grass, were groups of ballplayers, neatly dressed in uniforms, hitting fungoes and tossing baseballs back and forth.

"Hey fellas!" Moose exclaimed, turning to Pete and Eddie. "Looky over there. . . . It's Say-Hey!"

And sure enough, far beyond the outfield, chatting with one of his teammates between home plate and the Giants dugout, was Willie Mays! Pete took a deep breath and sat down as Willie trotted out toward him in center field. Then Willie turned to face the first Dodgers batter, and Pete felt a shiver pass through his body as he stared at the black-and-orange 24 on Willie's back.

"This can't be real!" he said, shaking his head . . . but deep down inside Pete knew that, of course, it was! That was Willie Mays standing right there, just beyond his fingertips!

The game was tied, 1–1, in the top of the eighth, when Carl Furillo hit a long blast that rocketed toward the outfield wall. In a split second Willie was after it. Racing into deep right center, he made one of his famous leaping catches, whirled, and threw a strike to home plate. His perfect peg nailed Billy Cox, who had tagged up at third and was trying to score the go-ahead run. Then Willie led off the bottom of the eighth with a clean single and scored the winning run when Wes Westrum launched a towering drive into the left-field grandstands. The crowd went wild, and Pete cheered until he nearly lost his voice.

FUNGO

Fungo is a style of hitting where the batter lobs the ball into the air and hits it. On the streets it refers to a type of stickball. In organized baseball, fungoes are hit during fielding practice by coaches using a very light bat made of balsa wood called a fungo bat.

After the game the Monarchs returned to the street and waited outside the clubhouse door . . . and after a while, Giants players began walking onto the sidewalk. First came Monte Irvin, then Bobby Thomson, and then . . . there was Willie! The Monarchs pushed through the crowd and stepped right up to him.

"Great game, Willie! We're gonna catch Dem Bums yet." Pete smiled.

Willie laughed, and patted Pete's head.

"Hey, Willie, we din't eat no lunch fer three days soz we could come see yuh play!" Moose added proudly. "We heard you wuz playin' stickball over in Harlem."

"Sure am," Willie chirped. "Actually, I'll be playin' down at 135th and Lenox in about half an hour."

"Well I guess we'll see yuh there!" Moose beamed.

"Say-hey . . . I'll be lookin' fo' you fellas." Willie winked.

THE SAY-HEY KID

Willie's manner of speech reflected that of the Deep South, where he grew up. When he got excited about something, Willie would often begin his sentences with the words *Say-hey*, and New Yorkers soon began calling him the Say-Hey Kid.

THE FIFTIES

During the 1950s, at least one New York team played in the World Series in nine out of ten years; and in five of those years, both teams were from New York! Every October, kids would go to school with transistor radios in their pockets. During class, they'd slip their earphones on, listening to the Series and passing the score written on folded pieces of paper to one another.

But the darkest days in New York baseball history also occurred in the fifties. On August 19, 1957, the Giants decided to leave the Big Apple, and then on October 8, 1957, Dodgers president Walter O'Malley announced that the beloved "Bums" would be following the "Jints" to the West Coast. That following April, the Yankees were the only team in town. Things stayed that way until 1962, when an expansion team called the Mets moved into New York.

In Harlem

WHEN THE MONARCHS ARRIVED, THE sidewalks of 135th Street were packed solid with people. Pete strained to get a look, but there were just too many bodies. He spotted a mail truck down the block and motioned to his teammates. Together, they squirmed through the crowd and climbed up onto the truck's roof.

From far down 135th Street, a cheer rose up from the multitude. Willie Mays stepped off the curb as a kid handed him a Spauldeen and a broomstick.

"Send it to the moon, Say-Hey!" Moose's voice boomed.

"Crush it, Willieee!" Eddie called out.

Pete just stood there, wide-eyed.

Willie stepped into the middle of 135th Street. He bounced the ball several times, and the crowd hushed. He lobbed it straight up, and the pink sphere rose,

THE CATCH

On September 29, 1954, Willie Mays made what is often regarded as the greatest catch in baseball history. It happened in the first game of the World Series. The Cleveland Indians had runners on first and second, and the score was tied, 2–2, when Vic Wertz hit a colossal drive to dead center field. Willie was after it with the crack of the bat. Racing straight back into the deepest part of the ballpark, Willie reached up and caught it over his shoulder more than 460 feet from home plate. Then he whirled and threw a perfect bullet to second base, preventing the Indians from scoring the go-ahead run.

From the broadcasting booth, it seemed to Jack Brickhouse that the long drive was a sure double or triple. When Willie made the unbelievable catch, Brickhouse announced to his listeners that it "must have been an optical illusion!"

STICKBALL LORE

Within days, word of Willie Mays's seven-sewer blast spread through the streets and sandlots of New York. Before long its status had been elevated to "legend." More than a half century later, Willie's blast is still discussed in the conversations of old stickball players. And if you're ever fortunate enough to meet one of the gray-headed sluggers, he'll usually swear that he saw Willie hit it with his own eyes.

hanging in midair for a split second. Willie cocked the broomstick, waiting motionless, and then he swung. There was a loud *pop*, and like a bullet, the Spauldeen shot up into the air. It grew smaller and smaller as it soared above the crowd, past row after row of apartment buildings, and finally landed behind some parked cars, disappearing far beyond the crowd.

"It's gotta be down that sewer!" Pete yelled, staring at the corner, and then began to count, "One, two, three, four, five . . . six . . . seven . . . Willie hit it seven sewers!"

"Impossa-bah-zool!" Moose sang out. "Nobody could hit a ball that far! The longest shot I ever seen was five sewuhs. . . . Seven? . . . No way, Say-Hey!"

"Well, maybe the ball broke the sound barrier and vaporized!" Eddie said, chuckling.

Pete kept staring at the spot where he'd seen the Spauldeen disappear.

"Nope," he insisted. "I'm positive. . . . It was seven sewers!"

The Monarchs waited as the sidewalks slowly emptied, and then they made their way along 135th Street. When they reached the sewer, Pete stared down into the blackness.

MIRIAM STREET

I learned about the use of wire coat hangers from Barry Kessler, an attorney who grew up in the Bronx. "We played on Miriam Street," Barry said, "on a hill between the Grand Concourse and Valentine Avenue. None of us had any money; but every spring, someone would show up with a can of paint and a brush, and the painting of the bases would begin: home plate at the top of the hill; second base near the bottom; first and third about fifteen feet apart, so that parked cars wouldn't cover them. We always painted two sets of bases, one for the little guys and a larger one for us. Once the stickball season began, Miriam Street would be packed. There were so many kids around that not only did you have two teams, but a cheering section as well."

THE RADIO BALL

Old stickball players tell stories of "the good ole days" when many a prodigy with major-league potential ruined his arm by throwing ninety-mile-per-hour fastballs in Wall Ball tournaments that lasted for days. One such prodigy was a kid named "Red" Pitkoff, who played at P.S. 84 on Gunhill Road in the North Bronx. Andy Liebman, a gym teacher who grew up in that neighborhood, told me all about him. "I never met a dude who could hit Red's fastball," Andy said. "The fact is, it was impossible to hit. It was called the Radio Ball by the local cats, because you could hear it but you couldn't see it!"

THE ETHICAL STICKBALL SOCIETY

On a Sunday in March 1973, in the town of Hastings-on-Hudson just north of the Bronx, a group of old stickball diehards met with broomsticks, tennis balls, and memories. They had a great time and decided to meet on the following Sunday. They kept playing until November, through heat waves, thunderstorms, and even a snow flurry. They soon had T-shirts made with the words *Eternal Summer* printed on them in Latin. They called themselves the Ethical Stickball Society, and they've been playing ever since. Among the original members were Stephan Kanfer, author of the best-selling book *Ball of Fire*; John Phillips, editor of the *International Herald Tribune*; Ray Kennedy of *Sports Illustrated*; and "Philadelphia" Phil Coltoff, CEO of the Children's Aid Society.

"PHILADELPHIA" PHIL

Though his nickname might fool you, Philadelphia Phil grew up in the Bronx, playing Wall Ball on the handball courts of Crotona Park. Possessing a sharp breaking curve and a blazing fastball, Phil pitched a no-hitter at the age of sixteen.

As an adult, Phil joined the Ethical Stickball Society. "The competition was intense," Phil told me, "but we never argued. A tremendous camaraderie developed between us. Over the years, we became good friends. After games, we'd go out for hot dogs and burgers, returning home late in the afternoon." Phil is the only player to hit a ball onto the roof of Hastings High School, a five-story building three hundred feet from home plate. He did this twice, once right-handed and once from the left side of the plate.

"I'm going down there," he said to Moose and Eddie. "Let's get the cover off." Together, the Monarchs lifted the metal grating. Pete pulled a folded wire coat hanger from his back pocket. He straightened it and formed a small loop at one end. Then Moose and Eddie each took hold of one of Pete's ankles, and they slowly lowered him into the foul-smelling sewer.

As Pete descended into the blackness, he took in a deep breath and began coughing.

"You aw-right, Buddy?" Moose called down to him.

THE MONARCHS AND THE LOAFERS

The Monarchs were a neighborhood stickball team that competed in the East Tremont section of the Bronx. Playing throughout the mid 1950s, the team was disbanded in 1957, when the players' families left the Bronx, moving to the northern suburbs. Pete Citrolo, one of the original Monarchs, talked with me about the two teams.

"The Monarchs played Slow Pitch on Vyse Avenue," Pete explained, "and there was an older group called the Loafers who played for money. It cost from one to five dollars a man, which in the fifties was big bucks to a twelve-year-old. Of course, I didn't have the money; but they were short a player, so one of the Loafers paid for me. I don't remember if we won or lost, but I was really scared . . . and I did get a couple of hits!"

"Yeah . . . sure," Pete answered between coughs. "I'm fine." He reached down with the hanger, searching through the black sewer bottom. Pete moved slowly and deliberately, making sure that he didn't miss a single spot. The loop of the hanger landed on something hard, and Pete lifted a soggy leather ball.

"Wrong ball," he mumbled to himself.

"You say sumpthin'?" Moose grunted.

"Nope . . . nothing," Pete answered.

He shook off the ball, slipped it into his pocket, and continued dragging the hanger through the slime, attempting to search every inch of the slippery sludge. Pete collected an awful-smelling rubber boot, a decaying magazine, and a pair of mud-covered shorts . . . but no Spauldeen.

"Are you finished yet?" Eddie called down. "My arm's killing me! . . . I can't hold on much longer."

"Okay . . . okay." Pete shrugged. "Get me outa here." His teammates lifted him out of the sewer, and Moose patted Pete on the back.

"You done your best, Buddy," Moose offered.

"Oh no . . . I didn't," Pete insisted. "I just missed it. I know it's still down there!"

THE MIRACLE OF COOGAN'S BLUFF

The legendary comeback of the 1951 Giants is referred to as the Miracle of Coogan's Bluff, the piece of high ground on the banks of the Harlem River where the Polo Grounds stood. With six and a half weeks to go in the season, the Dodgers held a thirteen-game lead over the Giants. Led by Willie Mays, the Giants swept the Dodgers in a three-game series in August. Going on to win sixteen games in a row, they caught the Dodgers on the next-to-the-last day of the season. A three-game play-off ensued; and going into the bottom of the ninth inning of the final game, the Giants trailed, 4–1. They narrowed the score to 4–2 with two singles and a double, when Bobby Thomson came to the plate and hit a line drive into the left-field grandstands. That home run is still referred to as the "Shot Heard Round the World."

ON THE 5 TRAIN

THE THREE BOYS TURNED AWAY from the sewer and climbed onto the elevated subway platform. A minute later they hopped onto the number 5 train.

As the subway rolled northward into the Bronx, Pete closed his eyes and thought back to the events of the day.

"Well, anyway, we did get to see Willie play," he said to himself, a smile spreading across his face. "And man . . . did he give that ball a ride . . . a seven-sewer ride!"

Remembering the sewer, Pete reached into his pocket and grasped the old hardball. He squeezed its soggy leather cover between his fingers. As he lifted it out of his pocket, a musty smell filled his nostrils. Pete held up the ball to the window. It was scratched all over and encrusted with dirt.

"It must have been down there a long time," Pete said to himself.

He found a crumpled piece of newspaper and began wiping away some of the grime. Looking closely at the ball, Pete noticed that there were handwritten words scribbled all over its leather cover. He scrubbed the ball again and struggled to read the words. They were written in script, all in pairs; and each pair of words had its own character, its own writing style.

Suddenly Pete's eyes narrowed as he remembered a tale his father used to tell.

"This just might be the ball!" Pete whispered as goose bumps covered his arms. Slowly rotating it between his fingers, he froze as he came upon a barely legible name.

"Hey, you guys! Get over here . . . right this second!" he demanded. "Take a look at this!"

Moose and Eddie gathered around Pete, and their mouths dropped open, for inscribed on the tattered leather cover of the ancient ball was the legendary signature of the greatest slugger of all time. And surrounding his name were the autographs of every other player on the team, a team whose lineup was once referred to as Murderers Row, the most awesome team in the history of baseball: the 1927 New York Yankees!

Maybe someday someone will find the Spauldeen.

SCORECARD

Thanks to Dora Socol, who was struck by a foul ball in the grandstands of Yankee Stadium in 1927 and brought into the Yankee clubhouse, where she was attended to by the team physician and given an autographed baseball signed by all the Yankee players; to Harold "Pops" Socol, who proudly told me the story of how he had swiped that ball and lost it down a sewer during a game with his friends; to Harold's lifelong buddy Lenny Workman, the real "Leonardo"; to Harold's and Lenny's wives, who really were both named Ruthie; to Pete Citrolo, who related the story of how he and his brother Bobby, along with Frankie and Gene Koerner and Ron Swern, created a stickball team they called the Monarchs during the 1950s; to my nephew, Andrew Clark, and his daughter Natalia, who posed before my camera as Bernard and Mona Finkel; and to my grandson, Nash Moses, who posed as the little leaguer who appears on the copyright page.

Further thanks to Gabriel Schechter, Claudette Burke, and Timothy J. Wiles of the Baseball Hall of Fame, who were so helpful during my hours in the research library in Cooperstown; to the fourth, fifth, and sixth graders of Green Mountain and Slater Elementary Schools in Golden, Colorado, and Roosevelt School in Hawthorne, New Jersey, who listened intently as I read the manuscript, asked me to make this a longer book, and suggested that I include a glossary of New York street terms.

Finally, I'd like to thank Jenny Shalant, Eric A. Kimmel, and my editor, Regina Griffin, whose sensitive readings of the manuscript were instrumental in the reimagining of the stories.